PUFFIN BOOKS

POEMS
for 9-Year-Olds and Under

Everyone grumbled. The sky was grey.
We had nothing to do and nothing to say.
We were nearing the end of a dismal day.
And there seemed to be nothing beyond,
Then
>   *Daddy fell into the pond!*

KIT WRIGHT was born in 1944 in Kent. He was educated at Berkhamsted school and New College, Oxford. He taught in a London Comprehensive and has spent three years lecturing in English Literature at Brook University, Ontario in Canada. He has also worked as Education Secretary to the Poetry Society in London, and been Fellow-Commoner in the Creative Arts at Trinity College, Cambridge. He now devotes all his time to poetry and is well known for his collections and anthologies, and as a performer and teacher.

POEMS
for 9-Year-Olds
and Under

CHOSEN BY KIT WRIGHT
ILLUSTRATED BY MICHAEL FOREMAN

Puffin Books

PUFFIN BOOKS

Published by the Penguin Group
Penguin Books Ltd, 27 Wrights Lane, London W8 5TZ, England
Penguin Books USA Inc., 375 Hudson Street, New York, New York 10014, USA
Penguin Books Australia Ltd, Ringwood, Victoria, Australia
Penguin Books Canada Ltd, 10 Alcorn Avenue, Toronto, Ontario, Canada M4V 3B2
Penguin Books (NZ) Ltd, 182–190 Wairau Road, Auckland 10, New Zealand

Penguin Books Ltd, Registered Offices: Harmondsworth, Middlesex, England

First published by Kestrel Books 1984
Published in Puffin Books 1985
9 10

Printed in England by Clays Ltd, St Ives plc
Filmset in Monophoto Palatino

Contents

ODD SORTS AND PECULIAR PARTIES

TRUE TRAVELS

STRANGE RELATIVES

BEAUTIFUL SOUP AND BIG BIG BURGERS

A MIGHTY BIG CATALOGUE OF MICE, BIRDS AND CATS

ANIMAL EXTRAS

DON'T BE SO SILLY

TIME TO REMEMBER

YOU COME
TOO

The Pasture

I'm going out to clean the pasture spring;
I'll only stop to rake the leaves away
(And wait to watch the water clear, I may):
I shan't be gone long. — You come too.

I'm going out to fetch the little calf
That's standing by the mother. It's so young
It totters when she licks it with her tongue.
I shan't be gone long. You come too.

ROBERT FROST

A Boy's Song

Where the pools are bright and deep,
Where the grey trout lies asleep,
Up the river and o'er the lea,
That's the way for Billy and me.

Where the blackbird sings the latest,
Where the hawthorn blooms the sweetest,
Where the nestlings chirp and flee,
That's the way for Billy and me.

Where the mowers mow the cleanest,
Where the hay lies thick and greenest;
There to trace the homeward bee,
That's the way for Billy and me.

Where the hazel bank is steepest,
Where the shadow falls the deepest,
Where the clustering nuts fall free,
That's the way for Billy and me.

Why the boys should drive away
Little sweet maidens from their play,
Or love to banter and fight so well,
That's the thing I never could tell.

But this I know, I love to play
Through the meadow, among the hay;
Up the water and o'er the lea,
That's the way for Billy and me.

JAMES HOGG

Jumper

When I was a lad as big as my Dad,
I jumped into a pea-pod;
Pea-pod was so full,
I jumped into a roaring bull;
Roaring bull was so fat,
I jumped into a gentleman's hat;
Gentleman's hat was so fine,
I jumped into a bottle of wine;
Bottle of wine was so clear,
I jumped into a bottle of beer;
Bottle of beer was so thick,
I jumped into a knobbed stick;
Knobbed stick wouldn't bend,
I jumped into a turkey hen;
Turkey hen wouldn't lay,
I jumped into a piece of clay;
Piece of clay was so nasty,
I jumped into an apple pasty;
Apple pasty was so good,
I jumped into a lump of wood;
Lump of wood was so rotten,
I jumped into a bale of cotton;
The bale of cotton set on fire,
Blew me up to Jeremiah;
Jeremiah was a prophet,
Had a horse and couldn't stop it;

Horse knocked against t'ould cobbler's door,
Knocked t'ould cobbler on the floor;
Cobbler with his rusty gun,
Shot the horse and off it run.

ANON.

In the Orchard

There was a giant by the Orchard Wall,
Peeping about on this side and on that,
And feeling in the trees. He was as tall
As the big apple tree, and twice as fat:
His beard poked out, all bristly-black, and there
Were leaves and gorse and heather in his hair.

He held a blackthorn club in his right hand,
And plunged the other into every tree,
Searching for something – You could stand
Beside him and not reach up to his knee,
So big he was – I trembled lest he should
Come trampling, round-eyed, down to where I stood.

I tried to get away. – But, as I slid
Under a bush, he saw me, and he bent
Down deep at me, and said, *'Where is she hid?'*
I pointed over there, and off he went –

But, while he searched, I turned and simply flew
Round to the lilac bushes back to you.

JAMES STEPHENS

Snake Glides

Snake glides
through grass
over
pebbles
forked tongue
working
never
speaking
but its
body
whispers
listen

KEITH BOSLEY

Who Has Seen the Wind?

Who has seen the wind?
Neither I nor you:
But when the leaves hang trembling,
The wind is passing through.

Who has seen the wind?
Neither you nor I:
But when the trees bow down their heads,
The wind is passing by.

CHRISTINA ROSSETTI

Snow

When winter winds blow
Hedges to and fro
And the flapping crow
Has gone to his home long ago,
Then I know
Snow
Will quietly fall, grow
Overnight higher than houses below,
Stop the stream in its flow,
And so
In a few hours, show
Itself man's ancient foe.
O
How slow
Is the silent gathering of snow.

LEONARD CLARK

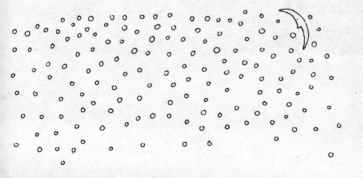

from
The Rain

Everywhere
The rain is falling
Through the air;
Brawling
On house and tree,
On every little place that you can see
The rain-drops go:
The roofs are wet, the walls, the ground below.

What can it be
That makes the high, wide heavens weep so bitterly?

JAMES STEPHENS

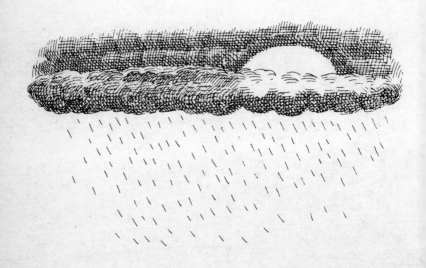

Nothing Else

There's nothing I can't see
From here,

There's nothing I can't be
From here.

Because my eyes
Are open wide
To let the big
World come inside,

I think I can see me
From here.

ELEANOR OLIPHANT

A POCKETFUL OF
RHYMES AND SONGS

W

The King sent for his wise men all
    To find a rhyme for W;
When they had thought a good long time
But could not think of a single rhyme,
    'I'm sorry,' said he, 'to trouble you.'

JAMES REEVES

An Epitaph

Beneath these high Cathedral stairs
Lie the remains of Susan Pares,
Her name was Wiggs it was not Pares
But Pares was put to rhyme with stairs.

EDWARD LEAR

A Poem Just Like This

Daddy came home and he read to me,
He read to me, he read to me,
Daddy came home and he read to me
A poem *just like this*!

Daddy came home and he said to me,
In bed to me, he said to me,
Daddy came home and he said to me
A poem *just like this*!

And then he gave me a kiss.

And then he said, 'Sleep tight!'

And then he put out the light.

BUT

You know, the other night ...

Daddy came home and he read to me,
In bed to me, he read to me,
Daddy came home and he read to me
And I didn't make a peep.

And before he'd finished the *poem like this*

And before he gave me a goodnight kiss

And before he said, 'Goodnight. Sleep tight!'

And before he got up and put out the light

Daddy was

Fast

Asleep!

GEORGE AND AUDREY MORTIMER-WATERFORD

The Writer of this Poem

The writer of this poem
Is taller than a tree
As keen as the North wind
As handsome as can be

As bold as a boxing-glove
As sharp as a nib
As strong as scaffolding
As tricky as a fib

As smooth as a lolly-ice
As quick as a lick
As clean as a chemist-shop
As clever as a

The writer of this poem
Never ceases to amaze
He's one in a million billion
(Or so the poem says!)

ROGER McGOUGH

The Key of the Kingdom

This is the Key of the Kingdom:
In that Kingdom there is a city;
In that city is a town;
In that town there is a street;
In that street there winds a lane;
In that lane there is a yard;
In that yard there is a house;
In that house there waits a room;
In that room an empty bed;
And on that bed a basket –
A basket of sweet flowers:
    Of flowers, of flowers;
    A basket of sweet flowers.

Flowers in a basket;
Basket on the bed;
Bed in the chamber;
Chamber in the house;
House in the weedy yard;
Yard in the winding lane;
Lane in the broad street;
Street in the high town;
Town in the city;
City in the Kingdom –
This is the Key of the Kingdom,
    Of the Kingdom this is the Key.

ANON.

Oliver Cromwell

Oliver Cromwell's buried and dead,
   He, hi, buried and dead.
There grew a ripe apple-tree over his head,
   He, hi, over his head.
The apples were ripe and ready to fall,
   He, hi, ready to fall.
There came an old woman and gathered them all,
   He, hi, gathered them all.
Oliver rose and gave her a clop,
   He, hi, gave her a clop,
Which made the old woman go hippertihop,
   He, hi, hippertihop.
Saddle and bridle are laid on the shelf,
   He, hi, laid on the shelf;
If you want any more you can sing it yourself,
   He, hi, sing it yourself.

ANON.

The Milkmaid

'Where are you going to, my Pretty Maid?'
'I'm going a-milking, Sir,' she said.

'Shall I go with you, my Pretty Maid?'
'Oh yes, if you please, kind Sir,' she said.

'What is your Father, my Pretty Maid?'
'My Father's a Farmer, Sir,' she said.

'Shall I marry you, my Pretty Maid?'
'Oh thank you kindly, Sir,' she said.

'But what is your Fortune, my Pretty Maid?'
'My face is my Fortune, Sir,' she said.

'Then I can't marry you, my Pretty Maid!'
'Nobody asked you, Sir!' she said.

'Nobody asked you, Sir!' she said.

'Sir!' she said.

ANON.

The Ceremonial Band

(To be said out loud by a chorus and solo voices)

The old King of Dorchester,
He had a little orchestra,
And never did you hear such a ceremonial band.
'Tootle-too,' said the flute,
'Deed-a-reedle,' said the fiddle,
For the fiddles and the flutes were the finest in the land.

The old King of Dorchester,
He had a little orchestra,
And never did you hear such a ceremonial band.
'Pump-a-rum,' said the drum,
'Tootle-too,' said the flute,
'Deed-a-reedle,' said the fiddle,
For the fiddles and the flutes were the finest in the land.

The old King of Dorchester,
He had a little orchestra,
And never did you hear such a ceremonial band.
'Pickle-pee,' said the fife,
'Pump-a-rum,' said the drum,
'Tootle-too,' said the flute,
'Deed-a-reedle,' said the fiddle,
For the fiddles and the flutes were the finest in the land.

The old King of Dorchester,
   He had a little orchestra,
And never did you hear such a ceremonial band.
   'Zoomba-zoom,' said the bass,
   'Pickle-pee,' said the fife,
   'Pump-a-rum,' said the drum,
   'Tootle-too,' said the flute,
   'Deed-a-reedle,' said the fiddle,
For the fiddles and the flutes were the finest in the land.

The old King of Dorchester,
   He had a little orchestra,
And never did you hear such a ceremonial band.
   'Pah-pa-rah,' said the trumpet.
   'Zoomba-zoom,' said the bass,
   'Pickle-pee,' said the fife,
   'Pump-a-rum,' said the drum,
   'Tootle-too,' said the flute,
   'Deed-a-reedle,' said the fiddle,
For the fiddles and the flutes were the finest in the land,
Oh! the fiddles and the flutes were the finest in the land!

JAMES REEVES

The tides to me,
the tides to me

The tides to me, the tides to me
   come dancing up the sand;
when the waves break I lean to take
   each one by the hand.

The tides from me, the tides from me
   roll backward down the shore.
I do not mind, for I shall find
   a thousand and one more.

GEORGE BARKER

Lightships

All night long when the wind is high
Nnn nnn nnnn
The lightships moan and moan to the sky
Nnn nnn nnnn.

Their foghorns whine when the mist runs free
Nnn nnn nnnn
Warning the men on the ships at sea
Nnn nnn nnnn.

CLIVE SANSOM

Chanson Innocente II

hist   whist
little ghostthings
tip-toe
twinkle-toe

little twitchy
witches and tingling
goblins
hob-a-nob   hob-a-nob

little hoppy happy
toad in tweeds
tweeds
little itchy mousies

with scuttling
eyes rustle and run and
hidehidehide
whisk

whisk look out for the old woman
with the wart on her nose
what she'll do to yer
nobody knows

for she knows the devil   ooch
the devil ouch
the devil
ach   the great

green
dancing
devil
devil

devil
devil

   wheeEE

            e. e. cummings

The Rabbit's Christmas Carol

I'm sick as a parrot,
I've lost me carrot,
I couldn't care less if it's
Christmas Day.

I'm sick as a parrot,
I've lost me carrot,
So get us a lettuce
Or ... go away!

KIT WRIGHT

A Legend of
Lake Okeefinokee

There once was a frog,
And he lived in a bog,
On the banks of Lake Okeefinokee.
And the words of the song
That he sang all day long
Were, 'Croakety croakety croaky.'

Said the frog, 'I have found
That my life's daily round
In this place is exceedingly poky.
So no longer I'll stop,
But I swiftly will hop
Away from Lake Okeefinokee.'

Now a bad mocking-bird
By mischance overheard
The words of the frog as he spokee.
And he said, 'All my life
Frog and I've been at strife,
As we lived by Lake Okeefinokee.

'Now I see at a glance
Here's a capital chance
For to play him a practical jokee.
So I'll venture to say
That he shall not to-day
Leave the banks of Lake Okeefinokee.'

So this bad mocking-bird,
Without saying a word,
He flew to a tree which was oaky;
And loudly he sang,
Till the whole forest rang,
'Oh! Croakety croakety croaky!'

As he warbled this song,
Master Frog came along,
A-filling his pipe for to smokee;
And he said, ''Tis some frog
Has escaped from the bog
Of Okeefinokee-finokee.

'I am filled with amaze
To hear one of my race
A-warbling on top of an oaky;
But if frogs can climb trees,
I may still find some ease
On the banks of Lake Okeefinokee.'

So he climbed up the tree:
But alas! down fell he!
And his lovely green neck it was brokee;
And the sad truth to say,
Never more did he stray
From the banks of Lake Okeefinokee.

And the bad mocking-bird
Said, 'How very absurd
And delightful a practical jokee!'
But I'm happy to say
He was drowned the next day
In the waters of Okeefinokee.

LAURA E. RICHARDS

ODD SORTS
AND
PECULIAR PARTIES

Mrs Snipkin
and Mrs Wobblechin

Skinny Mrs Snipkin,
With her little pipkin,
Sat by the fireside a-warming of her toes.
Fat Mrs Wobblechin
With her little doublechin,
Sat by the window a-cooling of her nose.

Says this one to that one,
'Oh! you silly fat one,
Will you shut the window down? You're freezing me to death!'
Says that one to t' other one,
'Good gracious, how you bother one!
There isn't air enough for me to draw my precious breath!'

Skinny Mrs Snipkin,
Took her little pipkin,
Threw it straight across the room as hard as she could throw;
Hit Mrs Wobblechin
On her little doublechin,
And out of the window a-tumble she did go.

LAURA E. RICHARDS

Bear

There was a boy
who almost saw
a bear beside
his bed.

O bear, what are
you looking for?
He almost went
and said;

And are you looking
for a boy
that's fat, and nicely
fed?

But then he shut
his eyes, and thought
of other things
instead.

JEAN KENWARD

Tom's Bomb

There was a boy whose name was Tom,
Who made a high explosive bomb,
By mixing up some iodine
With sugar, flour and plasticine.
Then, to make it smell more queer,
He added Daddy's home-made beer.
He took it off to school one day,
And when they all went out to play,
He left it by the radiator.
As the heat was getting greater,
The mixture in the bomb grew thick
And very soon it seemed to tick.
Miss Knight came in and gazed with awe
To see the bomb upon the floor.
'Dear me,' she said, 'it is a bomb,
An object worth escaping from.'
She went to Mr Holliday
And said in tones that were not gay,
'Headmaster, this is not much fun;
There is a bomb in Classroom One.'
'Great snakes,' said he, and gave a cough
And said, 'I hope it won't go off.
But on the off-chance that it does,
I think we'd better call the fuzz.'
A policeman came and said, 'Oh God,
We need the bomb disposal squad,
Some firemen and a doctor too,
A helicopter and its crew,

And, since I'm shaking in the legs,
A pot of tea and hard-boiled eggs.'
A bomb disposal engineer
Said, with every sign of fear,
'I've not seen one like that before,'
And rushed out, screaming, through the door.
Everyone became more worried
Till Tom, who seemed to be unflurried,
Asked what was all the fuss about?
'I'll pick it up and take it out.'
He tipped the contents down the drain
And peace and quiet reigned again.
Tom just smiled and shook his head
And quietly to himself he said:
'Excitement's what these people seek.
I'll bring another one next week.'

DAVID HORNSBY

Two Funny Men

I know a man
Who's upside down,
And when he goes to bed
His head's not on the pillow, No!
His *feet* are there instead.

I know a man
Who's back to front,
The strangest man *I've* seen.
He can't tell where he's going
But he knows where he has been.

SPIKE MILLIGAN

A Song of Toad

The world has held great Heroes,
  As history-books have showed;
But never a name to go down to fame
  Compared to that of Toad!

The clever men at Oxford
  Know all that there is to be knowed.
But they none of them know one half as much
  As intelligent Mr Toad!

The animals sat in the ark and cried,
  Their tears in torrents flowed.
Who was it said, 'There's land ahead'?
  Encouraging Mr Toad!

The Army all saluted
    As they marched along the road.
Was it the King? Or Kitchener?
    No. It was Mr Toad.

The Queen and her ladies-in-waiting
    Sat at the window and sewed.
She cried, 'Look! who's that *handsome* man?'
    They answered, 'Mr Toad.'

The motor-car went Poop-poop-poop
    As it raced along the road.
Who was it steered it into a pond?
    Ingenious Mr Toad!

KENNETH GRAHAME

Old Mrs Thing-um-e-bob

Old Mrs Thing-um-e-bob,
Lives at you-know-where,
Dropped her what-you-may-call-it down
The well of the kitchen stair.

'Gracious me!' said Thing-um-e-bob,
'This don't look too bright.
I'll ask old Mr What's-his-name
To try and put it right.'

Along came Mr What's-his-name,
He said, 'You've broke the lot!
I'll have to see what I can do
With some of the you-know-what.'

So he gave the what-you-may-call-it a pit
And he gave it a bit of a pat,
And he put it all together again
With a little of this and that.

And he gave the what-you-may-call-it a dib
And he gave it a dab as well
When all of a sudden he heard a note
As clear as any bell.

'It's as good as new!' cried What's-his-name.
'But please remember, now,
In future Mrs Thing-um-e-bob
You'll have to go you-know-how.'

CHARLES CAUSLEY

Up in a Basket

There was an old woman tossed up in a basket,
    Seventeen times as high as the moon;
And where she was going, I couldn't but ask it,
    For in her hand she carried a broom.
Old woman, old woman, old woman, quoth I,
    O whither, O whither, O whither so high?
To sweep the cobwebs off the sky!
    Shall I go with you? Aye, by-and-by.

ANON.

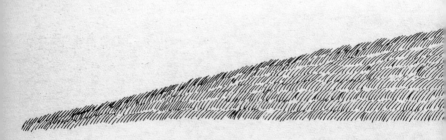

Down in a Bush

There was a man in our town,
   And he was wondrous wise,
He jumped into a bramble bush
   And scratched out both his eyes.
And when he saw his eyes were out,
   With all his might and main
He jumped into another bush
   And scratched them in again.

ANON.

Mud

I like mud.
　　I like it on my clothes.
I like it on my fingers.
　　I like it in my toes.

Dirt's pretty ordinary
　　And dust's a dud.
For a really good mess-up
　　I like mud.

JOHN SMITH

There was an old woman

There was an old woman who swallowed a fly;
I wonder why
She swallowed a fly.
Poor old woman, she's sure to die.

There was an old woman who swallowed a spider
That wriggled and jiggled and wriggled inside her.
She swallowed the spider to catch the fly,
I wonder why
She swallowed a fly.
Poor old woman, she's sure to die.

There was an old woman who swallowed a bird;
How absurd
To swallow a bird.
She swallowed the bird to catch the spider,
That wriggled and jiggled and wriggled inside her.
She swallowed the spider to catch the fly,
I wonder why
She swallowed a fly.
Poor old woman, she's sure to die.

There was an old woman who swallowed a cat;
Fancy that!
She swallowed a cat;
She swallowed the cat to catch the bird,
She swallowed the bird to catch the spider,
That wriggled and jiggled and wriggled inside her.

She swallowed the spider to catch the fly,
I wonder why
She swallowed a fly.
Poor old woman, she's sure to die.

There was an old woman who swallowed a dog;
Oh what a hog!
She swallowed a dog;
She swallowed the dog to catch the cat,
She swallowed the cat to catch the bird,
She swallowed the bird to catch the spider,
That wriggled and jiggled and wriggled inside her.
She swallowed the spider to catch the fly,
I wonder why
She swallowed a fly.
Poor old woman, she's sure to die.

There was an old woman who swallowed a cow;
I wonder how
She swallowed a cow;
She swallowed the cow to catch the dog,
She swallowed the dog to catch the cat,
She swallowed the cat to catch the bird,
She swallowed the bird to catch the spider,
That wriggled and jiggled and wriggled inside her.
She swallowed the spider to catch the fly,
I wonder why
She swallowed a fly.
Poor old woman, she's sure to die.

There was an old woman who swallowed a horse;
She died of course!

ANON.

A Party

On Willy's birthday, as you see,
These little boys have come to tea.
But, oh! how very sad to tell!
They have not been behaving well.
For ere they took a single bite,
They all began to scold and fight.

The little boy whose name was Ned,
He wanted jelly on his bread;
The little boy whose name was Sam,
He vowed he would have damson jam;
The little boy whose name was Phil
Said, 'I'll have honey! *Yes* – I – WILL!!'

BUT–

The little boy whose name was Paul,
While they were quarrelling, ate it all.

LAURA E. RICHARDS

My Party

My parents said I could have a party
And that's just what I did.

Dad said, 'Who had you thought of inviting?'
I told him. He said, 'Well, you'd better start writing,'
And that's just what I did

To:
Phyllis Willis, Horace Morris,
Nancy, Clancy, Bert and Gert Sturt,
Dick and Mick and Nick Crick,
Ron, Don, John,
Dolly, Molly, Polly –
Neil Peel –
And my dear old friend, Dave Dirt.

I wrote, 'Come along, I'm having a party,'
And that's just what they did.

They all arrived with huge appetites
As Dad and I were fixing the lights.
I said, 'Help yourself to the drinks and bites!'
And that's just what they did,
All of them:

Phyllis Willis, Horace Morris,
Nancy, Clancy, Bert and Gert Sturt,
Dick and Mick and Nick Crick,
Ron, Don, John,
Dolly, Molly, Polly –
Neil Peel –
And my dear old friend, Dave Dirt.

Now, I had a good time and as far as I could tell,
The party seemed to go pretty well –
Yes, that's just what it did.

Then Dad said, 'Come on, just for fun,
Let's have a *turn* from everyone!'
And a turn's just what they did,

All of them:

Phyllis Willis, Horace Morris,
Nancy, Clancy, Bert and Gert Sturt,
Dick and Mick and Nick Crick,
Ron, Don, John,
Dolly, Molly, Polly –
Neil Peel –
And my dear old friend, Dave Dirt.

AND THIS IS WHAT THEY DID:

Phyllis and Clancy
And Horace and Nancy
Did a song and dance number
That was really fancy –

Dolly, Molly, Polly,
Ron, Don and John
Performed a play
That went on and on and on –

Gert and Bert Sturt,
Sister and brother,
Did an imitation of
Each other.
(Gert Sturt put on Bert Sturt's shirt
And Bert Sturt put on Gert Sturt's skirt.)

Neil Peel
All on his own
Danced an eightsome reel.

Dick and Mick
And Nicholas Crick
Did a most *ingenious*
Conjuring trick

And my dear old friend, Dave Dirt,
Was terribly sick
All over the flowers.
We cleaned it up.
It took *hours*.

But as Dad said, giving a party's not easy.
You really
Have to
Stick at it.
I agree. And if Dave gives a party
I'm certainly
Going to be
Sick at it.

KIT WRIGHT

TRUE
TRAVELS

The Train to Glasgow

Here is the train to Glasgow.

Here is the driver,
Mr MacIver,
Who drove the train to Glasgow.

Here is the guard from Donibristle
Who waved his flag and blew his whistle
To tell the driver,
Mr MacIver,
To start the train to Glasgow.

Here is a boy called Donald MacBrain
Who came to the station to catch the train
But saw the guard from Donibristle
Wave his flag and blow his whistle
To tell the driver,
Mr MacIver,
To start the train to Glasgow.

Here is the guard, a kindly man
Who, at the last moment, hauled into the van
That fortunate boy called Donald MacBrain
Who came to the station to catch the train
But saw the guard from Donibristle
Wave his flag and blow his whistle
To tell the driver,
Mr MacIver,
To start the train to Glasgow.

Here are hens and here are cocks,
Clucking and crowing inside a box,
In charge of the guard, that kindly man
Who, at the last moment, hauled into the van
That fortunate boy called Donald MacBrain
Who came to the station to catch the train
But saw the guard from Donibristle
Wave his flag and blow his whistle
To tell the driver,
Mr MacIver,
To start the train to Glasgow.

Here is the train. It gave a jolt
Which loosened a catch and loosened a bolt,
And let out the hens and let out the cocks,
Clucking and crowing out of their box,
In charge of the guard, that kindly man
Who, at the last moment, hauled into the van
That fortunate boy called Donald MacBrain
Who came to the station to catch the train
But saw the guard from Donibristle
Wave his flag and blow his whistle.
To tell the driver,
Mr MacIver,
To start the train to Glasgow.

The guard chased a hen and, missing it, fell.
The hens were all squawking, the cocks were as well,
And unless you were there you haven't a notion
The flurry, the fuss, the noise and commotion
Caused by the train which gave a jolt
And loosened a catch and loosened a bolt

70

And let out the hens and let out the cocks,
Clucking and crowing out of their box,
In charge of the guard, that kindly man
Who, at the last moment, hauled into the van
That fortunate boy called Donald MacBrain
Who came to the station to catch the train
But saw the guard from Donibristle
Wave his flag and blow his whistle
To tell the driver,
Mr MacIver,
To start the train to Glasgow.

Now Donald was quick and Donald was neat
And Donald was nimble on his feet.
He caught the hens and he caught the cocks
And he put them back in their great big box.
The guard was pleased as pleased could be
And invited Donald to come to tea
On Saturday, at Donibristle,
And let him blow his lovely whistle,
And said in all his life he'd never
Seen a boy so quick and clever,
And so did the driver,
Mr MacIver,
Who drove the train to Glasgow.

WILMA HORSBRUGH

If Pigs Could Fly

If pigs could fly, I'd fly a pig
To foreign countries small and big –
To Italy and Spain,
To Austria, where cowbells ring,
To Germany, where people sing –
And then come home again.

I'd see the Ganges and the Nile;
I'd visit Madagascar's isle,
And Persia and Peru.
People would say they'd never seen
So odd, so strange an air-machine
As that on which I flew.

Why, everyone would raise a shout
To see his trotters and his snout
Come floating from the sky;
And I would be a famous star
Well known in countries near and far –
If only pigs could fly!

JAMES REEVES

The Jumblies

I

They went to sea in a Sieve, they did,
   In a Sieve they went to sea:
In spite of all their friends could say,
On a winter's morn, on a stormy day,
   In a Sieve they went to sea!
And when the Sieve turned round and round,
And every one cried, 'You'll all be drowned!'
They called aloud, 'Our Sieve ain't big,
But we don't care a button! we don't care a fig!
   In a Sieve we'll go to sea!'
     Far and few, far and few,
       Are the lands where the Jumblies live;
      Their heads are green, and their hands are blue,
       And they went to sea in a Sieve.

II

They sailed away in a Sieve, they did,
   In a Sieve they sailed so fast,
With only a beautiful pea-green veil
Tied with a riband by way of a sail,
   To a small tobacco-pipe mast;
And every one said, who saw them go,
'O won't they be soon upset, you know!
For the sky is dark, and the voyage is long,
And happen what may, it's extremely wrong

In a Sieve to sail so fast!'
   Far and few, far and few,
      Are the lands where the Jumblies live;
    Their heads are green, and their hands are blue,
      And they went to sea in a Sieve.

III

The water it soon came in, it did,
   The water it soon came in;
So to keep them dry, they wrapped their feet
In a pinky paper all folded neat,
   And they fastened it down with a pin.
And they passed the night in a crockery-jar,
And each of them said, 'How wise we are!
Though the sky be dark, and the voyage be long,
Yet we never can think we were rash or wrong,
   While round in our Sieve we spin!'
    Far and few, far and few,
      Are the lands where the Jumblies live;
    Their heads are green, and their hands are blue,
      And they went to sea in a Sieve.

IV

And all night long they sailed away;
   And when the sun went down,
They whistled and warbled a moony song
To the echoing sound of a coppery gong,
   In the shade of the mountains brown.
'O Timballo! How happy we are,

When we live in a Sieve and a crockery-jar,
And all night long in the moonlight pale,
We sail away with a pea-green sail,
   In the shade of the mountains brown!'
      Far and few, far and few,
         Are the lands where the Jumblies live;
         Their heads are green, and their hands are blue,
            And they went to sea in a Sieve.

V

They sailed to the Western Sea, they did,
   To a land all covered with trees,
And they bought an Owl, and a useful Cart,
And a pound of Rice, and a Cranberry Tart,
   And a hive of silvery Bees.
And they bought a Pig, and some green Jack-daws,
And a lovely Monkey with lollipop paws,
And forty bottles of Ring-Bo-Ree,
   And no end of Stilton Cheese.
      Far and few, far and few,
         Are the lands where the Jumblies live;
         Their heads are green, and their hands are blue,
            And they went to sea in a Sieve.

VI

And in twenty years they all came back,
   In twenty years or more,
And every one said, 'How tall they've grown!

For they've been to the Lakes, and the Torrible Zone,
   And the hills of the Chankly Bore;'
And they drank their health, and gave them a feast
Of dumplings made of beautiful yeast;
And every one said, 'If we only live,
We too will go to sea in a Sieve, —
   To the hills of the Chankly Bore!'
    Far and few, far and few,
     Are the lands where the Jumblies live;
    Their heads are green, and their hands are blue,
     And they went to sea in a Sieve.

EDWARD LEAR

What someone said
when he was spanked on the day
before his birthday

Some day
I may
Pack my bag and run away.
Some day
I may.
— But not today.

Some night
I might
Slip away in the moonlight.
I might.
Some night.
— But not tonight.

Some night.
Some day.
I might.
I may.
— But right now I think I'll stay.

JOHN CIARDI

The Black Pebble

There went three children down to the shore,
    Down to the shore and back;
There was skipping Susan and bright-eyed Sam
    And little scowling Jack.

Susan found a white cockle-shell,
    The prettiest ever seen,
And Sam picked up a piece of glass
    Rounded and smooth and green.

But Jack found only a plain black pebble
    That lay by the rolling sea,
And that was all that ever he found;
    So back they went all three.

The cockle-shell they put on the table,
    The green glass on the shelf,
But the little black pebble that Jack had found,
    He kept it for himself.

JAMES REEVES

Buckingham Palace

They're changing guard at Buckingham Palace –
Christopher Robin went down with Alice.
Alice is marrying one of the guard.
'A soldier's life is terrible hard,'
                                    Says Alice.

They're changing guard at Buckingham Palace –
Christopher Robin went down with Alice.
We saw a guard in a sentry-box.
'One of the sergeants looks after their socks,'
                                    Says Alice.

They're changing guard at Buckingham Palace –
Christopher Robin went down with Alice.
We looked for the King, but he never came.
'Well, God take care of him, all the same,'
                                    Says Alice.

They're changing guard at Buckingham Palace –
Christopher Robin went down with Alice.
They've great big parties inside the grounds.
'I wouldn't be King for a hundred pounds,'
                                    Says Alice.

They're changing guard at Buckingham Palace –
Christopher Robin went down with Alice.
A face looked out, but it wasn't the King's.
'He's much too busy a-signing things,'
                              Says Alice.

They're changing guard at Buckingham Palace –
Christopher Robin went down with Alice.
'Do you think the King knows all about *me*?'
'Sure to, dear, but it's time for tea,'
                              Says Alice.

A. A. MILNE

Going through the World

as I was running
   up the down escalator
I passed Jeff Nuttall
   running down the up

TOM PICKARD

Up-hill

Does the road wind up-hill all the way?
   Yes, to the very end.
Will the day's journey take the whole long day?
   From morn to night, my friend.

But is there for the night a resting-place?
   A roof for when the slow dark hours begin.
May not the darkness hide it from my face?
   You cannot miss that inn.

Shall I meet other wayfarers at night?
   Those who have gone before.
Then must I knock or call when just in sight?
   They will not keep you standing at the door.

Shall I find comfort, travel-sore and weak?
   Of labour you shall find the sum.
Will there be beds for me and all who seek?
   Yea, beds for all who come.

CHRISTINA ROSSETTI

STRANGE RELATIVES

Daddy Fell into the Pond

Everyone grumbled. The sky was grey.
We had nothing to do and nothing to say.
We were nearing the end of a dismal day.
And there seemed to be nothing beyond,
> Then
>> Daddy fell into the pond!

And everyone's face grew merry and bright,
And Timothy danced for sheer delight.
'Give me the camera, quick, oh quick!
He's crawling out of the duckweed!' Click!

Then the gardener suddenly slapped his knee,
And doubled up, shaking silently,
And the ducks all quacked as if they were daft,
And it sounded as if the old drake laughed.
Oh, there wasn't a thing that didn't respond
> When
>> Daddy fell into the pond!

ALFRED NOYES

My Dad, Your Dad

My dad's fatter than your dad,
Yes, my dad's fatter than yours:
If he eats any more he won't fit in the house,
He'll have to live out of doors.

Yes, but my dad's balder than your dad,
My dad's balder, O.K.,
He's only got two hairs left on his head
And both are turning grey.

Ah, but my dad's thicker than your dad,
My dad's thicker, all right.
He has to look at his watch to see
If it's noon or the middle of the night.

Yes, but my dad's more boring than your dad.
If he ever starts counting sheep
When he can't get to sleep at night, he finds
It's the sheep that go to sleep.

But my dad doesn't mind your dad.
Mine quite likes yours too.
I suppose they don't always think much of US!
That's true, I suppose, that's true.

KIT WRIGHT

The Reverend Sabine Baring-Gould

The Reverend Sabine Baring-Gould,
   Rector (sometime) at Lew,
Once at a Christmas party asked,
   'Whose pretty child are you?'

(The Rector's family was long,
   His memory was poor,
And as to who was who had grown
   Increasingly unsure).

At this, the infant on the stair
   Most sorrowfully sighed.
'Whose pretty little girl am I?
   Why, *yours*, papa!' she cried.

CHARLES CAUSLEY

Disobedience

James James
Morrison Morrison
Weatherby George Dupree
Took great
Care of his Mother,
Though he was only three.
James James
Said to his Mother,
'Mother,' he said, said he;
'You must never go down to the end of the town,
   if you don't go down with me.'

James James
Morrison's Mother
Put on a golden gown,
James James
Morrison's Mother
Drove to the end of the town.
James James
Morrison's Mother
Said to herself, said she:
'I can get right down to the end of the town and be
   back in time for tea.'

King John
Put up a notice,
'LOST or STOLEN or STRAYED!
JAMES JAMES
MORRISON'S MOTHER
SEEMS TO HAVE BEEN MISLAID.
LAST SEEN
WANDERING VAGUELY:
QUITE OF HER OWN ACCORD,
SHE TRIED TO GET DOWN TO THE END OF
   THE TOWN – **FORTY SHILLINGS REWARD!**

James James
Morrison Morrison
(Commonly known as Jim)
Told his
Other relations
Not to go blaming *him*.
James James
Said to his Mother,
'Mother,' he said, said he:
'You must *never* go down to the end of the town
    without consulting me.'

James James
Morrison's mother
Hasn't been heard of since.
King John
Said he was sorry,
So did the Queen and Prince.
King John
(Somebody told me)
Said to a man he knew:
'If people go down to the end of the town, well, what
    can *anyone do*?'

(Now then, very softly)

J. J.
M. M.
W. G. Du P.
Took great
C/o his M*****
Though he was only 3.
J. J.
Said to his M*****
'M*****,' he said, said he:

'You-must-never-go-down-to-the-end-of-the-town-if-
    you-don't go-down-with ME!'

A. A. MILNE

Speak roughly
to your little boy

Speak roughly to your little boy
 And beat him when he sneezes:
He only does it to annoy,
 Because he knows it teases.

CHORUS
Wow! wow! wow!

I speak severely to my boy,
 I beat him when he sneezes;
For he can thoroughly enjoy
 The pepper when he pleases!

CHORUS
Wow! wow! wow!

LEWIS CARROLL

The Quarrel

I quarrelled with my brother
I don't know what about,
One thing led to another
And somehow we fell out.
The start of it was slight,
The end of it was strong,
He said he was right,
I knew he was wrong!

We hated one another.
The afternoon turned black.
Then suddenly my brother
Thumped me on the back,
And said, 'Oh, *come* along!
We can't go on all night –
I was in the wrong.'
So he was in the right.

ELEANOR FARJEON

Old Mrs Lazibones

Old Mrs Lazibones
And her dirty daughter
Never used soap
and never used water.

Higgledy piggledy cowpat
What d'you think of that?

Daisies from their fingernails,
Birds' nests in their hair-O,
Dandelions from their ears, –
What a dirty pair-O!

Higgledy piggledy cowpat
What d'you think of that?

Came a prince who sought a bride,
Riding past their doorstep,
Quick, said Mrs Lazibones.
Girl, under the watertap.

Higgledy piggledy cowpat
What d'you think of that?

Washed her up and washed her down,
Then she washed her sideways,
But the prince was far, far away,
He'd ridden off on the highways.

Higgledy piggledy cowpat
What d'you think of that?

GERDA MAYER

Railings

towards the end of his tether
grandad
at the drop of a hat
would paint the railings

overnight
we became famous
allover the neighbourhood
for our smart railings

(and our dirty hats)

ROGER MCGOUGH

My Sister Laura

My sister Laura's bigger than me
And lifts me up quite easily.
I can't lift her, I've tried and tried;
She must have something heavy inside.

SPIKE MILLIGAN

from
Aunts and Uncles

When Aunty Jane
Became a Crane
She put one leg behind her head;
And even when the clock struck ten
Refused to go to bed.

When Aunty Grace
Became a Plaice
She all but vanished sideways on;
Except her nose
And pointed toes
The rest of her was gone.

When Aunty Jill
Became a Pill
She stared all day through dark-blue glass;
And always sneered
When men appeared
To ask her how she was.

When Uncle Jake
Became a Snake
He never found it out;
And so as no one mentions it
One sees him still about.

MERVYN PEAKE

Night Starvation or The Biter Bit

At night my Uncle Rufus
(Or so I've heard it said)
Would put his teeth into a glass
Of water by his bed.

At three o'clock one morning
He woke up with a cough,
And as he reached out for his teeth —
They bit his hand right off.

CAREY BLYTON

Uncle John

Uncle John
Has a sit-upon
That is large
And round
And fat

And the car
Of his choice
Is an old
Rolls-Royce
So he drives

About
In
That!

Yes, Uncle J.,
I have to say,
Has a huge
And wide
Backside,

So in
That car
He drives
So far,

There isn't any room for anyone else to ride!

RONALD WRIGHT

BEAUTIFUL SOUP
AND
BIG BIG BURGERS

Poem on Bread

The poet is about to write a poem;
He does not use a pencil or a pen.
He dips his long thin finger into jam
Or something savoury preferred by men.
This poet does not choose to write on paper;
He takes a single slice of well-baked bread
And with his jam or Marmite-nibbed forefinger
He writes his verses down on that instead.
His poem is fairly short as all the best are.
When he has finished it he hopes that you
Or someone else – your brother, friend or sister –
Will read and find it marvellous and true.
If you can't read, then eat: it tastes quite good.
If you do neither, all that I can say
Is he who needs no poetry or bread
Is really in a devilish bad way.

VERNON SCANNELL

Beautiful Soup

Beautiful Soup, so rich and green,
Waiting in a hot tureen!
Who for such dainties would not stoop?
Soup of the evening, beautiful Soup!
Soup of the evening, beautiful Soup!
    Beau – ootiful Soo – oop!
    Beau – ootiful Soo – oop!
Soo – oop of the e – e – vening,
    Beautiful, beautiful Soup!

Beautiful Soup! Who cares for fish,
Game, or any other dish?
Who would not give all else for two p
ennyworth only of beautiful Soup?
Pennyworth only of beautiful Soup?
    Beau – ootiful Soo – oop!
    Beau – ootiful Soo – oop!
Soo – oop of the e – e – vening,
    Beautiful beauti – FUL SOUP!

LEWIS CARROLL

The King's Breakfast

The King asked
The Queen, and
The Queen asked
The Dairymaid:
'Could we have some butter for
The Royal slice of bread?'
The Queen asked
The Dairymaid,
The Dairymaid
Said, 'Certainly,
I'll go and tell
The cow
Now
Before she goes to bed.'

The Dairymaid
She curtsied,
And went and told
The Alderney:
'Don't forget the butter for
The Royal slice of bread.'
The Alderney
Said sleepily:
'You'd better tell
His Majesty
That many people nowadays
Like marmalade
Instead.'

The Dairymaid
Said, 'Fancy!'
And went to
Her Majesty.
She curtsied to the Queen, and
She turned a little red:
'Excuse me,
Your Majesty,
For taking of
The liberty,
But marmalade is tasty, if
It's very
Thickly
Spread.'

The Queen said
'Oh!'
And went to
His Majesty:
'Talking of the butter for
The royal slice of bread,
Many people
Think that
Marmalade
Is nicer.
Would you like to try a little
Marmalade
Instead?'

The King said,
'Bother!'
And then he said,
'Oh, deary me!'
The King sobbed, 'Oh, deary me!'
And went back to bed.
'Nobody,'
He whimpered,
'Could call me
A fussy man;
I *only* want
A little bit
Of butter for
My bread!'

The Queen said,
'There, there!'
And went to
The Dairymaid.
The Dairymaid
Said, 'There, there!'
And went to the shed.
The cow said,
'There, there!
I didn't really
Mean it;
Here's milk for his porringer
And butter for his bread.'

The Queen took
The butter
And brought it to
His Majesty;
The King said,
'Butter, eh?'
And bounced out of bed.
'Nobody,' he said,
As he kissed her
Tenderly,
'Nobody,' he said,
As he slid down
The banisters,
'Nobody,
My darling,
Could call me
A fussy man –
BUT
I do like a little bit of butter to my bread!'

A. A. MILNE

On Nevski Bridge

On Nevski Bridge a Russian stood,
Chewing his beard for lack of food.
Said he, 'It's tough, this stuff, to eat
But a darned sight better than shredded wheat!'

ANON.

Mustard

I'm mad about mustard –
Even on custard.

OGDEN NASH

THE HARDEST THING TO DO
IN THE WORLD
is stand in the hot sun
at the end of a long queue for ice creams
watching all the people who've just bought theirs
coming away from the queue
giving their ice creams their very first lick.

MICHAEL ROSEN

The Friendly
Cinnamon Bun

Shining in his stickiness and glistening with honey,
Safe among his sisters and his brothers on a tray,
With raisin eyes that looked at me as I put down my money,
There smiled a friendly cinnamon bun, and
    this I heard him say:

'It's a lovely, lovely morning, and the world's a
    lovely place;
I know it's going to be a lovely day.
I know we're going to be good friends; I like
    your honest face;
Together we might go a long, long way.'

The baker's girl rang up the sale, 'I'll wrap your
    bun,' said she.
'Oh no, you needn't bother,' I replied.
I smiled back at that cinnamon bun and ate
    him, one two three,
And walked out with his friendliness inside.

RUSSELL HOBAN

There was an old man

There was an old man
Had a face made of cake,
He stuck it with currants
And put it in to bake.

The oven was hot,
He baked it too much,
It came out covered
With a crunchy crust.

The eyes went pop,
The currants went bang,
And that was the end
Of that old man.

JAMES KIRKUP

Tom's Little Dog

Tom told his dog called Tim to beg,
And up at once he sat,
His two clear amber eyes fixed fast,
His haunches on his mat.

Tom poised a lump of sugar on
His nose; then, 'Trust!' says he;
Stiff as a guardsman sat his Tim;
Never a hair stirred he.

'Paid for!' says Tom; and in a trice
Up jerked that moist black nose;
A snap of teeth, a crunch, a munch,
And down the sugar goes!

WALTER DE LA MARE

I Think I'll Go and Eat Worms

Nobody loves me,
Everybody hates me,
I think I'll go and eat worms.
Great big fat ones,
Long thin skinny ones,

And the gravy goes
SLURP SLURP SLURP SLURP.

ANON.

The Cabbage

The cabbage is a funny veg.
All crisp, and green, and brainy.
I sometimes wear one on my head
When it's cold and rainy.

ROGER McGOUGH

Bitter Butter

Betty Botter bought some butter,
But, she said, this butter's bitter;
If I put it in my batter,
It will make my batter bitter,
But a bit of better butter
Will make my batter better.
So she bought a bit of butter
Better than her bitter butter,
And she put it in her batter,
And it made her batter better,
So 'twas better Betty Botter
Bought a bit of better butter.

ANON.

A Tongue Twister

If he could sell her salt
I could sell her a salt-cellar
for salt for her celery

MICHAEL ROSEN

Jerry Hall

Jerry Hall,
He is so small,
A rat could eat him,
Hat and all.

ANON.

A MIGHTY
BIG CATALOGUE
OF MICE,
BIRDS AND CATS

The Original
and Vastly Superior Song
of Three Blind Mice

Three Small Mice
Three Small Mice
Three Small Mice

Pined for some fun
Pined for some fun
Pined for some fun

They made up their minds to set out to roam;
Said they, ''Tis dull to remain at home,'
And all the luggage they took was a comb,
   These three Small Mice.

Three Bold Mice
Three Bold Mice
Three Bold Mice

Came to an Inn
Came to an Inn
Came to an Inn

'Good evening, Host, can you give us a bed?'
But the Host he grinned and he shook his head;
So they all slept out in a field instead,
   These three Bold Mice.

Three Cold Mice
Three Cold Mice
Three Cold Mice

Woke up next morn
Woke up next morn
Woke up next morn

They each had a cold and swollen face
Through sleeping all night in an open space;
So they rose quite early and left the place,
    These three Cold Mice.

Three Hungry Mice
Three Hungry Mice
Three Hungry Mice

Searched for some food
Searched for some food
Searched for some food

But all they found was a walnut shell
That lay by the side of a dried-up well;
Who had eaten the nut they could not tell,
    These three Hungry Mice.

Three Starved Mice
Three Starved Mice
Three Starved Mice

Came to a Farm
Came to a Farm
Came to a Farm

The Farmer was eating some bread and cheese,
So they all went down on their hands and knees
And squeaked, 'Pray give us a morsel, please,'
     These three Starved Mice.

Three Glad Mice
Three Glad Mice
Three Glad Mice

Ate all they could
Ate all they could
Ate all they could

They felt so happy they danced with glee
But the Farmer's Wife came in to see
What might this merry-making be
     Of three Glad Mice.

Three Poor Mice
Three Poor Mice
Three Poor Mice

Soon changed their tune
Soon changed their tune
Soon changed their tune

The Farmer's Wife said, 'What are you at,
And why are you capering round like that?
Just wait a minute: I'll fetch the Cat!'
    Oh dear! Poor Mice.

Three Scared Mice
Three Scared Mice
Three Scared Mice

Ran for their lives
Ran for their lives
Ran for their lives

They jumped out on to the window ledge,
The mention of 'Cat' set their teeth on edge;
So they hid themselves in the bramble hedge
    These three Scared Mice.

Three Sad Mice
Three Sad Mice
Three Sad Mice

What could they do?
What could they do?
What could they do?

The bramble hedge was most unkind:
It scratched their eyes and made them blind
And soon each Mouse went out of his mind,
    These three Sad Mice.

Three Blind Mice
Three Blind Mice
Three Blind Mice

See how they run
See how they run
See how they run

They all ran after the Farmer's Wife,
Who cut off their tails with a carving knife.
Did you ever see such a thing in your life
    As three Blind Mice?

Three Sick Mice
Three Sick Mice
Three Sick Mice

Gave way to tears
Gave way to tears
Gave way to tears

They could not see and they had no end;
They sought a Chemist and found a Friend;
He gave them some 'Never Too Late To Mend',
    These three Sick Mice.

Three Wise Mice
Three Wise Mice
Three Wise Mice

Rubbed, rubbed away
Rubbed, rubbed away
Rubbed, rubbed away

And soon their tails began to grow,
And their eyes recovered their sight, you know;
They looked in the glass and it told them so,
  These three Wise Mice.

Three Proud Mice
Three Proud Mice
Three Proud Mice

Soon settled down
Soon settled down
Soon settled down

The name of their house I cannot tell;
But they've learnt a trade and are doing well;
If you call upon them, ring the bell
  Three times twice.

ANON.

Death of a Mouse

A mouse returning late one night
Happy, or mildly drunk,
Danced a gavotte by the pale moonlight.
An owl caught sight of him.
Clunk.

JAMES FENTON

He Was a Rat

He was a rat, and she was a rat,
    And down in one hole they did dwell,
And both were as black as a witch's cat,
    And they loved each other well.

He had a tail, and she had a tail,
    Both long and curling and fine;
And each said, 'Yours is the finest tail
    In the world, excepting mine.'

He smelt the cheese, and she smelt the cheese,
    And they both pronounced it good;
And both remarked it would greatly add
    To the charms of their daily food.

So he ventured out, and she ventured out,
    And I saw them go with pain;
But what befell them I never can tell,
    For they never came back again.

ANON.

Sid the Rat

Sid was a rat
Who kept a hat shop,
Ordinary sort of stuff:

Pork pies,
Panamas,
Old flat caps,
Bowlers,
Boaters
For old fat chaps,
Deerstalkers,
Stetsons ...
And that was *enough*
For *that* shop!

Yes, Sid was a rat
Who kept a hat shop,
Ordinary sort of trade:

Eels,
Elks,
Dirty old foxes,
Skinny
Kittens
In travelling boxes,
Elephants,
Owls ...
And business *paid*
In *that* shop!

One day the Mayor knocked on the door,
Said, 'Sid, you can't stay here no more!
We're going to knock your hat shop down
To build a new road through the town!'

'Is that a fact?'
Said Sid the Rat,
'Is that a fact?'
Said he.
'We'll see!

You build your road and I'll get my hats
And I'll stack them up like a block of flats

Right in the middle
And hey-diddle-diddle!
The cars won't know
Which way to go!
And I'll get the elk
And the dirty old fox
And the kitten
Out of her travelling box
And the slithering eel
And the wise owl too
And the elephant
On his way to the zoo
And I'll tell you what they'll do!

They'll pull those drivers out
Willy-nilly
And they'll tickle those drivers
And tickle them silly!
There'll be *huge* traffic jams
But they won't care!
So how do you like THAT,
Mr Mayor?'

'Oh,' said the Mayor.
'Oh dear,' said the Mayor.
'Hum,' said the Mayor.
'I fear,' said the Mayor,

You'd better keep your hat shop, Sid,
And carry on the way you did!'

Sid

Did!

ELEANOR OLIPHANT

from
The Swallow

Pretty swallow, once again
Come and pass me in the rain.
Pretty swallow, why so shy?
Pass again my window by.

Pretty little swallow, fly
Village doors and windows by,
Whisking o'er the garden pales
Where the blackbird finds the snails;

On yon low-thatched cottage stop,
In the sooty chimney pop,
Where thy wife and family
Every evening wait for thee.

JOHN CLARE

The Old False Leg

Three crows hopped on an old false leg,
   On an old false leg,
   An old false leg,
Three crows hopped on an old false leg
   Which lay out alone on the moor.

Whoever could have dropped that old false leg,
   Old false leg,
   That old false leg,
Whoever could have dropped that old false leg
   Out by the lake on the moor?

It was nobody dropped that old false leg,
   Old false leg,
   Old false leg,
It was nobody dropped that very false leg,
   Which slept out alone on the moor.

That old false leg jumped up on its toes,
   Up on its toes,
   Up on its toes,
That old false leg jumped up on its toes,
   In the very wet mist on the moor,

And it hit the tail feathers off those crows,
   Off those crows,
   Off those crows,
And it hit the tail feathers off those crows,
   Caw, caw, caw on the moor.

And those crows flew away quite nakedly,
   Quite nakedly,
   Quite nakedly,
And those crows flew away quite nakedly,
   Into the mist on the moor.

And the false leg thereupon strolled to the shore,
   Strolled to the shore,
   Strolled to the shore,
And the false leg thereupon strolled to the shore,
   Into the lake, and was seen no more.

GEOFFREY GRIGSON

Self-Pity

I never saw a wild thing
sorry for itself.
A small bird will drop frozen dead from a bough
without ever having felt sorry for itself.

D. H. LAWRENCE

The Blackbird

In the far corner,
Close by the swings,
Every morning
A blackbird sings.

His bill's so yellow,
His coat's so black,
That he makes a fellow
Whistle back.

Ann, my daughter,
Thinks that he
Sings for us two
Especially.

HUMBERT WOLFE

The Canary

The song of canaries
Never varies,
And when they're molting
They're pretty revolting.

OGDEN NASH

'Arry's 'Awk

'Arry 'ad an 'awk in an 'atbag
  An' the 'awk made an 'orrible row.
'Arry 'it the 'awk wiv an 'eavy 'ard 'ammer.
  'Arry ain't got an 'awk now.

ANON.

Cats

Those who love cats which do not even purr,
Or which are thin and tired and very old,
Bend down to them in the street and stroke their fur
And rub their ears and smooth their breast, and hold
Their paws, and gaze into their eyes of gold.

FRANCIS SCARFE

Catalogue

Cats sleep fat and walk thin.
Cats, when they sleep, slump;
When they wake, pull in —
And where the plump's been
There's skin.
Cats walk thin.

Cats wait in a lump,
Jump in a streak.
Cats, when they jump, are sleek
As a grape slipping its skin —
They have technique.
Oh, cats don't creak.
They sneak.

Cats sleep fat.
They spread comfort beneath them
Like a good mat,
As if they picked the place
And then sat.
You walk around one
As if he were the City Hall
After that.

If male,
A cat is apt to sing upon a major scale:
This concert is for everybody, this
Is wholesale.
For a baton, he wields a tail.

A cat condenses.
He pulls in his tail to go under bridges,
And himself to go under fences.
Cats fit
In any size box or kit;
And if a large pumpkin grew under one,
He could arch over it.

When everyone else is just ready to go out,
The cat is just ready to come in.
He's not where he's been.
Cats sleep fat and walk thin.

ROSALIE MOORE

This and That

Two cats together
In bee-heavy weather
After the August day
In smug contentment lay
By the garden shed
In the flower bed
Yawning out the hours
In the shade of the flowers
And passed the time away,
Between stretching and washing and sleeping,
Talking over the day.

'Climbed a tree.'
'Aaaah.'
'Terrorized sparrows.'
'Mmmmh.'
'Was chased.'
'Aaaah.'
'Fawned somewhat!'
'Mmmmh.'
'Washed, this and that,'
Said the first cat.

And they passed the time away
Between stretching and washing and sleeping
Talking over the day.

'Gazed out of parlour window.'
'Aaaah.'
'Pursued blue bottles.'
'Mmmmh.'
'Clawed curtains.'
'Aaaah.'
'Was cuffed.'
'Mmmmh.'
'Washed, this and that.'
Said the other cat.

And they passed the time away
Between stretching and washing and sleeping
Talking over the day.

'Scratched to be let in.'
'Aaaah.'
'Patrolled the house.'
'Mmmmh.'
'Scratched to go out.'
'Aaaah.'
'Was booted.'
'Mmmmh.'
'Washed, this and that.'
Said the first cat.

And they passed the time away
Between stretching and washing and sleeping
Talking over the day.

'Lapped cream elegantly.'
'Aaaah.'
'Disdained dinner.'
'Mmmmh.'
'Borrowed a little salmon.'
'Aaaah.'
'Was tormented.'
'Mmmmh.'
'Washed, this and that.'
Said the other cat.

And they passed the time away
Between stretching and washing and sleeping
Talking over the day.

GARETH OWEN

The Rum Tum Tugger

The Rum Tum Tugger is a Curious Cat.
If you offer him pheasant he would rather have grouse.
If you put him in a house he would much prefer a flat,
If you put him in a flat then he'd rather have a house.
If you set him on a mouse then he only wants a rat,
If you set him on a rat then he'd rather chase a mouse.
Yes the Rum Tum Tugger is a Curious Cat —
     And there isn't any call for me to shout it:
          For he will do
          As he do do
               And there's no doing anything about it!

The Rum Tum Tugger is a terrible bore:
When you let him in then he wants to be out;
He's always on the wrong side of every door,
And as soon as he's at home, then he'd like to get about.
He likes to lie in the bureau drawer,
But he makes such a fuss if he can't get out.
Yes the Rum Tum Tugger is a Curious Cat —
     And there isn't any use for you to doubt it:
          For he will do
          As he do do
               And there's no doing anything about it!

The Rum Tum Tugger is a curious beast:
His disobliging ways are a matter of habit.
If you offer him fish then he always wants a feast;
When there isn't any fish then he won't eat rabbit.
If you offer him cream then he sniffs and sneers,
For he only likes what he finds for himself;
So you'll catch him in it right up to the ears,
If you put it away on the larder shelf.
The Rum Tum Tugger is artful and knowing,
The Rum Tum Tugger doesn't care for a cuddle;
But he'll leap on your lap in the middle of your sewing,
For there's nothing he enjoys like a horrible muddle.
Yes the Rum Tum Tugger is a Curious Cat —
    And there isn't any need for me to spout it:
        For he will do
        As he do do
            And there's no doing anything about it!

T. S. ELIOT

My Uncle Paul of Pimlico

My Uncle Paul of Pimlico
Has seven cats as white as snow,
Who sit at his enormous feet
And watch him, as a special treat,
Play the piano upside-down,
In his delightful dressing-gown;
The firelight leaps, the parlour glows,
And, while the music ebbs and flows,
They smile (while purring the refrains),
At little thoughts that cross their brains.

MERVYN PEAKE

ANIMAL
EXTRAS

The Beauties of Britain

England is full of terrible uglies
(Don't mention Scotland, Ireland or Wales!) –
many of them have faces like horses
and some look like snails
and leave vapour trails!

Britain is full of horrible uglies
(Don't mention highways, byeways or roads!) –
many of them look like Pekineses
and some look like toads,
in their mean abodes!

Britain is full to the brim with uglies
(Don't mention islands, highlands or lakes!) –
many of them have heads like horse-flies
or half-baked cakes –
they're Nature's mistakes!

GAVIN EWART

The Pobble
Who Has No Toes

I

The Pobble who has no toes
  Had once as many as we;
When they said, 'Some day you may lose them all;' —
  He replied, — 'Fish fiddle de-dee!'
And his Aunt Jobiska made him drink
Lavender water tinged with pink,
For she said, 'The World in general knows
There's nothing so good for a Pobble's toes!'

II

The Pobble who has no toes,
  Swam across the Bristol Channel;
But before he set out he wrapped his nose
  In a piece of scarlet flannel.
For his Aunt Jobiska said. 'No harm
Can come to his toes if his nose is warm;
And it's perfectly known that a Pobble's toes
Are safe, — provided he minds his nose.'

III

The Pobble swam fast and well
   And when boats or ships came near him
He tinkledy-binkledy-winkled a bell
   So that all the world could hear him.
And all the Sailors and Admirals cried,
When they saw him nearing the further side, —
'He has gone to fish, for his Aunt Jobiska's
Runcible Cat with crimson whiskers!'

IV

But before he touched the shore,
   The shore of the Bristol Channel,
A sea-green Porpoise carried away
   His wrapper of scarlet flannel.
And when he came to observe his feet
Formerly garnished with toes so neat
His face at once became forlorn
On perceiving that all his toes were gone!

V

And nobody ever knew
   From that dark day to the present,
Whoso had taken the Pobble's toes,
   In a manner so far from pleasant.
Whether the shrimps or crawfish gray,
Or crafty Mermaids stole them away —
Nobody knew; and nobody knows
How the Pobble was robbed of his twice five toes!

VI

The Pobble who has no toes
    Was placed in a friendly Bark,
And they rowed him back, and carried him up,
    To his Aunt Jobiska's Park.
And she made him a feast at his earnest wish
Of eggs and buttercups fried with fish; —
And she said, — 'It's a fact the whole world knows,
That Pobbles are happier without their toes.'

EDWARD LEAR

The Truth about
the Abominable Footprint

The Yeti's a Beast
Who lives in the East
    And suffers a lot from B.O.
His hot hairy feet
Stink out the street
    So he cools them off in the snow.

MICHAEL BALDWIN

The Marrog

My desk's at the back of the class
And nobody, nobody knows
I'm a Marrog from Mars
With a body of brass
And seventeen fingers and toes.
Wouldn't they shriek if they knew
I've three eyes at the back of my head
And my hair is bright purple
My nose is deep blue
And my teeth are half-yellow, half-red?
My five arms are silver and spiked
With knives on them sharper than spears.
I could go back right now, if I liked –
And return in a million light-years.
I could gobble them all
For I'm seven foot tall
And I'm breathing green flames from my ears.
Wouldn't they yell if they knew,
If they guessed that a Marrog was here?
Ha-ha they haven't a clue –
Or wouldn't they tremble with fear!
'Look, look, a Marrog'
They'd all scream – and SMACK
The blackboard would fall and the ceiling would crack
And the teacher would faint, I suppose.
But I grin to myself, sitting right at the back
And nobody, nobody knows.

R. C. SCRIVEN

Ode to an Extinct Dinosaur

Iguanadon, I loved you,
With all your spiky scales,
Your massive jaws,
Impressive claws
And teeth like horseshoe nails.

Iguanadon, I loved you.
It moved me close to tears
When first I read
That you've been dead
For ninety million years.

DOUG MACLEOD

Multikertwigo

I saw the Multikertwigo
Standing on his head,
He was looking at me sideways
And this is what he said:
'Sniddle Iddle Ickle Thwack
Nicki — Nacki — Noo
Biddle — diddle Dicky — Dack
Tickle — tockle — too!'
None of this made sense to me,
Maybe it does to you.

SPIKE MILLIGAN

The Vampire

The night is still and sombre,
and in the murky gloom,
arisen from his slumber,
the vampire leaves his tomb.

His eyes are pools of fire,
his skin is icy white,
and blood his one desire
this woebegotten night.

Then through the silent city
he makes his silent way,
prepared to take no pity
upon his hapless prey.

An open window beckons,
he grins a hungry grin,
and pausing not one second
he swiftly climbs within.

JACK PRELUTSKY

The Derby Ram

As I went down to Derby town,
  'Twas on a market day,
And there I met the finest ram
  Was ever fed on hay.
    Riddle to my rye,
    Riddle to my rye.

The wool upon this ram's back,
  It grew up to the sky;
The eagles build their nests in it,
  I heard the young ones cry.
    Riddle to my rye,
    Riddle to my rye.

The horns upon this ram's head,
  They grew up to the moon.
A man climbed up in April
  And never came down till June.
    Riddle to my rye,
    Riddle to my rye.

The wool upon this ram's tail
  Was very fine and thin,
Took all the girls in Derby town
  Full seven years to spin.
    Riddle to my rye,
    Riddle to my rye.

This ram he had four mighty feet
   And on them he did stand,
And every foot that he had got
   Did cover an acre of land.
     Riddle to my rye,
     Riddle to my rye.

And every tooth this ram had
   Was hollow as a horn.
They took one out and measured it.
   It held a barrel of corn.
     Riddle to my rye,
     Riddle to my rye.

And if you don't believe me
   And think it is a lie,
Then you go down to Derby town
   And see as well as I.
     Riddle to my rye,
     Riddle to my rye.

ANON.

DON'T
BE
SO SILLY

Twinkle, Twinkle, Little Bat

Twinkle, twinkle, little bat!
How I wonder what you're at!
Up above the world you fly,
Like a tea-tray in the sky.
       Twinkle, twinkle –
Twinkle, twinkle, twinkle, twinkle.

LEWIS CARROLL

On the Ning Nang Nong

On the Ning Nang Nong
Where the Cows go Bong!
And the Monkeys all say Boo!
There's a Nong Nang Ning
Where the trees go Ping!
And the tea pots Jibber Jabber Joo.
On the Nong Ning Nang
All the mice go Clang!
And you just can't catch 'em when they do!
So it's Ning Nang Nong!
Cows go Bong!
Nong Nang Ning!
Trees go Ping!
Nong Ning Nang!
The mice go Clang!
What a noisy place to belong,
Is the Ning Nang Ning Nang Nong!!

SPIKE MILLIGAN

Somebody said that it Couldn't be Done

Somebody said that it couldn't be done —
But he, with a grin, replied
He'd not be the one to say it couldn't be done —
Leastways, not 'til he'd tried.
So he buckled right in, with a trace of a grin;
By golly, he went right to it.
He tackled The Thing That Couldn't Be Done
And he couldn't do it.

ANON.

Don't Stare

In the dark park
A crocus croaked
And a duck ducked

A spider eyed her
As he hunted
For serpentigers

Somewhere a tree barked
And a flock of geese
Creased the sun

I watched my watch
'Don't stare at me' it said
So I got up and left

Or was it right?

WILLIAM MORRISON BELL

Invisible

It wasn't a sudden thing;
There were no falling stars
Or choirs of voices;
No rushes of wind
Or flashes of lightning;
I simply woke up one morning
And wasn't there.
Or at least
I knew I was there
But there wasn't anything to be seen
That you might have called me.
If anybody had been there they would have seen
A huge smile of pride creasing my face
That is if I had a face
For a smile to crease on.
It hadn't been easy;
Every day for nearly a year
I'd been trying to persuade my body
To have second thoughts
About being there.
In quiet corners unobserved
I'd order my body
To go away.
'Go away body,' I'd say
But my body seemed to need more convincing.
Down I'd look
And there it would still be
Being there all over the place.

I had a very stubborn body
Where being there was concerned.
But now all that effort
Seemed to be worthwhile.
I'm not saying I didn't have
Little doubts.
For example I said to myself,
'If you're not there anymore
Where are you?'
Or to put it another way,
How could I know
I wasn't there
If I wasn't there?
After a bit
All this thinking
Started to make my head ache,
That is if I'd had a HEAD
To make aches with.
I got up out of bed
Put my clothes on my invisible body
Washed my invisible face,
Brushed my invisible teeth
And took my invisible self on a walk
To meet the world.
It would be a day to remember
I promised myself.
What fun I thought
I'll have with my sister,
The postman,

The school librarian,
And my haughty teacher with the spectacles,
Miss Simpkins.
But
Although I told them
I was invisible
Nobody would believe
What they couldn't see
In front of their own eyes.
When the jug poured milk
As if by magic,
Instead of falling down
Into a faint with amazement
My sister said,
'You'll be late for school.'
The gate pushed open
By an unseen hand;
But the postman only said,
'Two letters for you.'
Books flew unaided into the shelves;
'What a helpful boy,'
Said the librarian;
Spellings wrote themselves
Across my exercise book,
'Could do better,'
Wrote Miss Simpkins
In haughty red handwriting.
When I shouted at them all,
'I'm invisible,

I'm invisible,
Look at me I'm invisible,'
They all smiled
The same tight-lipped smile.
They don't know
That they can't see me.

GARETH OWEN

Nutter

The moon's a big white football,
The sun's a pound of butter.
The earth is going round the twist
And I'm a little nutter!

KIT WRIGHT

Poet-tree

I remember a tree
Upon a hill.
If it stood there then,
Does it stand there still?

If it doesn't stand still
And moves about,
Then open the gates
And let it out!

SPIKE MILLIGAN

TIME
TO
REMEMBER

Mrs Moon

Mrs Moon
sitting up in the sky
Little Old Lady
rock-a-bye
with a ball of fading light
and silvery needles
knitting the night.

ROGER MCGOUGH

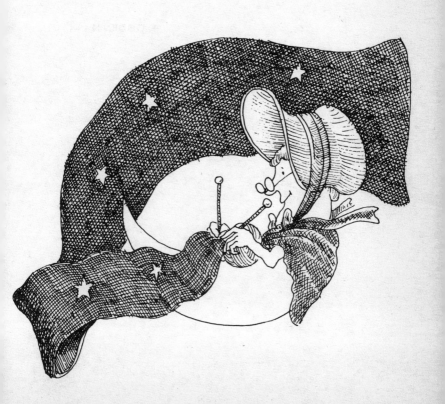

Sweet Dreams

I wonder as into bed I creep
What it feels like to fall asleep.
I've told myself stories, I've counted sheep,
But I'm always asleep when I fall asleep.
Tonight my eyes I will open keep,
And I'll stay awake till I fall asleep,
Then I'll know what it feels like to fall asleep,
Asleep,
Asleeep,
Asleeeep ...

OGDEN NASH

In This City

In this city, perhaps a street.
In this street, perhaps a house.
In this house, perhaps a room.
And in this room a woman sitting,
Sitting in the darkness, sitting and crying
For someone who has just gone through the door
And who has just switched off the light
Forgetting she was there.

ALAN BROWNJOHN

Salford Road

Salford Road, Salford Road,
Is the place where I was born,
With a green front gate, a red brick wall
And hydrangeas round a lawn.

Salford Road, Salford Road,
Is the road where we would play
Where the sky lay over the roof tops
Like a friend who'd come to stay.

The Gardeners lived at fifty-five,
The Lunds with the willow tree,
Mr Pool with the flag and the garden pond
And the Harndens at fifty-three.

There was riding bikes and laughing
Till we couldn't laugh any more,
And bilberries picked on the hillside
And picnics on the shore.

I lay in bed when I was four
As the sunlight turned to grey
And heard the train through my pillow
And the seagulls far away.

And I rose to look out of my window
For I knew that someone was there
And a man stood as sad as nevermore
And didn't see me there.

And when I stand in Salford Road
And think of the boy who was me
I feel that from one of the windows
Someone is looking at me.

My friends walked out one Summer day,
Walked singing down the lane,
My friends walked into a wood called Time
And never came out again.

We live in a land called Gone-Today
That's made of bricks and straw
But Salford Road runs through my head
To a land called Evermore.

GARETH OWEN

It Was Long Ago

I'll tell you, shall I, something I remember?
Something that still means a great deal to me.
It was long ago.

A dusty road in summer I remember,
A mountain, and an old house, and a tree
That stood, you know,

Behind the house. An old woman I remember
In a red shawl with a grey cat on her knee
Humming under a tree.

She seemed the oldest thing I can remember,
But then perhaps I was not more than three.
It was long ago.

I dragged on the dusty road, and I remember
How the old woman looked over the fence at me
And seemed to know

How it felt to be three, and called out, I remember
'Do you like bilberries and cream for tea?'
I went under the tree

And while she hummed, and the cat purred, I remember
How she filled a saucer with berries and cream for me
So long ago,

Such berries and such cream as I remember
I never had seen before, and never see
Today, you know.

And that is almost all I can remember,
The house, the mountain, the grey cat on her knee,
Her red shawl, and the tree,

And the taste of the berries, the feel of the sun I remember,
And the smell of everything that used to be
So long ago,

Till the heat on the road outside again I remember,
And how the long dusty road seemed to have for me
No end, you know.

That is the farthest thing I can remember.
It won't mean much to you. It does to me.
Then I grew up, you see.

ELEANOR FARJEON

Index of First Lines

Index of Poets

Acknowledgements

The editor and publishers gratefully acknowledge permission to reproduce copyright poems in this book.

'The tides to me, the tides to me' by George Barker, reprinted by permission of Faber and Faber Ltd from *Runes and Rhymes and Tunes and Chimes* by George Barker; 'Night Starvation *or* the Biter Bit' by Carey Blyton, reprinted by permission of Faber and Faber Ltd from *Bananas in Pyjamas* by Carey Blyton; 'Snake Glides' by Keith Bosley, reprinted by permission of the author; 'In This City' by Alan Brownjohn from *Collected Poems 1952–1983*, reprinted by permission of the author and Secker and Warburg Ltd; 'The Reverend Sabine Baring-Gould' and 'Old Mrs Thing-um-e-bob' by Charles Causley from *Figgie Hobbin*, reprinted by permission of the author, Macmillan and David Higham Associates; 'What someone said when he was spanked on the day before his birthday' by John Ciardi, reprinted by permission of J. B. Lippincott & Co.; 'Snow' by Leonard Clark, reprinted by permission of the author; 'Chanson Innocente II' by e. e. cummings from *Selected Poems 1960*, reprinted by permission of Hart Davis MacGibbon, Granada Publishing Ltd; 'Tom's Little Dog' by Walter de la Mare, reprinted by permission of the Literary Trustees of Walter de la Mare and The Society of Authors as their representative; 'The Rum Tum Tugger' by T. S. Eliot, reprinted by permission of Faber and Faber Ltd from *Old Possum's Book of Practical Cats* by T. S. Eliot; 'The Beauties of Britain' by Gavin Ewart, reprinted by permission of the author; 'It was Long Ago' and 'The Quarrel' by Eleanor Farjeon from *Silver Sand and Snow*, reprinted by permission of Michael Joseph and David Higham Associates; 'Death of a Mouse' by James Fenton, reprinted by permission of the author; 'The Pasture' by Robert Frost from *The Poetry of Robert Frost*, edited by Edward Connery Lathem, reprinted by permission of the Estate of Robert Frost, the editor and Jonathan Cape Ltd and by permission of Holt, Rinehart and Winston Inc.; 'The Old False Leg' by Geoffrey Grigson, reprinted by permission of the author; 'The Friendly Cinnamon Bun' by Russell Hoban, reprinted by permission of the author; 'The Train to Glasgow' by Wilma Horsbrugh, reprinted by permission of the author; 'Bear' by Jean Kenward, reprinted by permission of the author; 'There was an old man' by James Kirkup, reprinted by permission of the